What Readers Are Saying

If you're looking for a supplemental course of study to meet the needs of your students, then I highly recommend Dr. Robbie Johnson's soft skills curriculum—education that goes above and beyond the core academic standards. As an educator, I witnessed firsthand the curriculum's positive impact on students and how it enhanced students' communication skills and the ability to collaborate within teams. Today's workforce is looking for employees who exhibit the ability to interact with colleagues using interpersonal skills currently not taught in the school system. Dr. Johnson's research and insightful analysis of the importance of interpersonal skills is sure to prove beneficial in any educational setting.

—Yvette Hubbard, Educator

A champion of accountability and positive self-actualization, Dr. Johnson's curriculum provides a framework that guides students toward an improved quality of life directly related to accessing the tools necessary to improve the quality of their decisions.

—Sylvia Stitt Smith, Facilitator of Relationship Education and Leadership Certification (REAL Essentials)

Before the Application and Beyond

and Beyond

CREATING MY LIFE PROFILE

Robbie Johnson, Ph.D.

MYND
MATTERS

Books may be purchased in bulk quantity and/or special sales by contacting the publisher.

Published by Mynd Matters Publishing
715 Peachtree Street NE
Suites 100 & 200
Atlanta, GA 30308
www.myndmatterspublishing.com

ISBN: 978-1-957092-39-3

FIRST EDITION

CONTENTS

Preface

Entering the workplace for the first time or changing employers can simultaneously be exciting and cause for anxiety. For the first-time job seeker, *Before the Application and Beyond* provides integral tools, strengthens skills, heightens awareness, and challenges internal and external assumptions through the use of case studies.

Spotlighting communication, teamwork, and personal accountability, this curriculum aims to familiarize students with expectations and requirements of the workforce and raise awareness of the interdependence of learning and skills development. Whether it is a first job or a change in career, preparation is always in order. *Before the Application and Beyond* prepares you to move from where you are, to the next level.

INTRODUCTION

Employers have expressed concern that educational systems are not adequately preparing students for the workforce. Globalization has created a culturally diverse workforce, and technological improvements have changed the skills required to accomplish business tasks. Such changes affect how students learn in preparation for the work experience. Soft skills, also known as personal skills, interpersonal skills, and transferable skills, are essential because of the required interaction with other people—coworkers, teams, and customers. These foundational skills are referenced as prime areas of opportunity. Employers have expressed concern that high school graduates with diplomas do not meet the minimum employability requirements.

The U. S. Department of Labor Secretary's Commission on Achieving Necessary Skills (SCANS), has identified workplace know-how competencies and foundational skills for employment. The report is recognized as a seminal document in workforce preparation.

SCANS Workplace Know-How

The Foundation Competence

Basic Skills	Reading, writing, arithmetic, mathematics, listening, speaking.
Thinking Skills	Thinking creatively, making decisions, solving problems, seeing things in the mind's eye, knowing how to learn, and reasoning.
Personal Skills	Individual responsibility, self-esteem, sociability, self-management, and integrity.

Five Competencies

Resources	Allocating time, money, materials, space, and staff;
Interpersonal Skills	Working on teams, teaching others, serving customers, leading, negotiating, and working well with people from culturally-diverse backgrounds;

Information	Acquiring and evaluating data, organizing and maintaining files, interpreting and communicating, and using computers to process information;
Systems	Understanding social, organizational, and technological systems, monitoring and correcting performance, and designing or improving systems;
Technology	Selecting equipment and tools, applying technology to specific tasks, and maintaining and troubleshooting technologies.

The curriculum strategy is to contextualize and integrate formal and informal learning before the application and show the influences on the hiring process. Long before an application is a thought, an individual has created a profile online and personal interactions that reveal critical information to future and prospective employers. That profile is the accumulation of choices, both direct and indirect, and the result of those choices often determine the outcome of gainful employment.

Before the Application and Beyond focuses on workforce education and readiness skills to prepare for work environment entrances. Identifying and addressing problematic behaviors that may not transfer into a work environment early-on—consistent tardiness, chronic absenteeism, and poor job performance—allows one to avoid cause for disciplinary action that could include or lead to termination.

Soft skills are the ability to navigate and adapt to everyday life situations. Efficiency depends on the level of a given skill. Soft skills include decision-making, problem-solving, literacy, critical thinking, empathy, interpersonal skills, assertiveness (confidence), self-awareness, and self-management. The settings that will test the application of these skills are relationships in the family, friendships, school, organizations, and the workplace.

Each individual will bring some influence from the culture that formed and shaped them into the corporate environment. It is essential to make a distinction. Merriam-Webster defines culture as characteristic features of a way of life, beliefs, values, and attitudes shared by people in a place or time. A second definition is corporare culture which is the shared attitudes, values, goals, and practices that characterize an institution or organization. The terms shared attitudes, values, and goals may not align in a definition for both groups.

Introduction

Throughout this curriculum are intentional challenges. They allow you to pause and look at self for a reality check. You can also gain an understanding of the profile you are creating as you evaluate the level of skills and potential adjustments that may be needed.

The implementation methodology starts with students writing a one-page essay titled My Life After High School. The essay allows for individual difference, the process of planning to reach the destination is similar. The exercise requires reading and writing, two basic skills. Some careers require college, some do not. If college is a desire, even as an athlete, what subjects and GPA are needed for admission? If seeking scholarships essays and interviewing skills are needed.

The essay serves as an instrument for the planning process.

Describe the profession you desire.

What type of skills are needed?

If college is needed, identify at least three that offer the degree needed.

What is the admission requirement of each?

If college is not needed, what type of training is needed?

Where can you get the training?

What classes are needed now?

Are you committed to do your best in your present classes?

Even if the context of the essay changes, the skills in planning, asking questions and researching is learned.

MODULE 1: LIFE SKILLS

Module Description

Soft and life skills provide the ability to navigate and adapt to everyday encounters. Soft skills, also referred to as people skills, characterize how people interact with others. These skills are essential for long-term success because each phase of life presents a different group of people for engagement. The content of this module is designed to demonstrate the synergy of the skills.

Learning Objectives – Choices and Consequences

1. Understand that choices have consequences (results)
2. Recognize choices are the core of creating one's life profile
3. Recognize that choices are not isolated and consequences profoundly impact self and others
4. Identify and interpret the interdependency of all life skills

Choices

Before an application is a thought, an individual is creating a profile through choices that will reveal crucial information to a prospective employer. Results from that profile will be included as information in a background check, credit check, and qualifications needed in the future. A recruiter makes conclusions regarding the type of employee a person will make for a company based on their profile.

In this module, students will review soft skills and life skills that influence the outcome of one's life.

A person's life is an all-inclusive accumulation of choices and consequences. Options begin every morning, starting with waking up. Do your feet hit the floor immediately if the alarm clock rings, or do you hit the snooze button? How many times will the snooze be selected, and what is the cost of snoozing? Notice that after a choice is made, behavior follows. By choosing to snooze, is breakfast missed? Is transportation missed? Are you late getting to your destination? Are you taking lunch? If so, is it prepared and ready to go? Are you eating out today? If so, how much will it cost? Can you afford to eat out? Do you have everything needed for the day? These are examples of possible choices based on one choice—to snooze or not to snooze—and you have yet to leave home. The responsibility of the decision belongs to the decision-maker.

All choices have consequences (results) that create an outcome with rippling effects, potentially impacting others and different areas of one's life. The ripple effect means that the results have the potential to influence and impact others. Details of circumstances determine the magnitude of choice; however, something that appears insignificant can have a significant impact when making a choice. Using the previous example of starting the day, what if the destination is an appointment? If it is a doctor's appointment, lateness may require rescheduling for another time because other people may have appointments already scheduled after you. If the first person is late, it could cause delays with other patients. What if it was a job interview? Being late could terminate consideration for being hired because of a negative impression. What if the destination was school? Class instruction is missed, affecting learning, and learning is required for course completion. This is the ripple effect, and when minors are involved, parents are included in the ripple effect.

There is a potential for the ripple effect to continue generationally. An example is not having crucial conversations. Critical discussions are composed of difficult, truthful, factual, and necessary exchanges. It is another way of addressing "the elephant" in the room and communicating what is wrong without sugar-coating, blaming, and camouflaging it. Some ripple effects are cultural because of the attitude that it is easier not to address the problem or the problem may be embedded in a belief or value. Give careful thought to the consequences and costs when making decisions.

The statement "I didn't have a choice" is a fallacy. While, it may sound appropriate, doing nothing is still a choice. Perhaps the implication is not having preferred options from which to choose. How do you make decisions? Do you have a process? Be cautious of using popularity as a high or only measurement in decision-making because popularity does not give validity, determine right or wrong, or determine if something is appropriate. Popularity as a measurement can be detrimental. Thinking or saying that "everybody" is doing _____ (whatever it is) is misleading because exceptions make that statement false and the justification unacceptable.

Be mindful of the people that are in your circle of influence. Your circle of influence includes the people you are constantly with and whom you may call friends. How do you define "friend"? Does the definition describe those closest to you? Stop and evaluate the influence of your friends. Is it a positive or negative impact? Which of the following describe most conversations with your inner circle? Are they healthy, encouraging, uplifting, kind, and supportive to do and be your best, or unhealthy, harmful, or self-destructive? Your friends and associates could be the measure used to interpret your reputation.

Who has the most significant impact on you and your decisions?

Internet / Social Media Choices

Internet behavior is a choice. Be careful what you post, which is another opportunity for the ripple effect. Words matter and can derail dreams and desires. Because of internet posting decisions, people have lost employment, school admissions, and job offers. What is on the internet does not disappear.

The internet has excellent popularity. However, universities and employers check the internet for digital footprints. Individuals may claim freedom of speech and the right to post whatever they desire. Businesses and organizations maintain the independence to protect their brand and reputation by vetting those who will represent the company or organization. Their products and customers are essential. Internet postings indicate something about the poster's character, which becomes part of the poster's profile. Remember, choices create one's profile.

The following case studies are not fictional. The content is based on actual events from a newspaper or other media source. Real consequences (results) were experienced because of the choices made in each case study. Analyze, discuss, and pay attention to the cost of the choices.

Exercise: After reading the case study:

Identify the decision-maker(s).
What was the decision?
What was the consequence(s)?
What was the ripple effect?
List the lessons learned from the case.
Notice the attitude of the decision-maker and others involved.

Case Study I

Harvard Rescinds Acceptances for At Least Ten Students for Obscene Memes
By Hannah Natanson, Crimson Staff Writer June 5, 2017
https://www.thecrimson.com/article/2017/6/5/2021-offers-rescinded-memes

Harvard College rescinded admissions offers to at least ten prospective members of the Class of 2021 after the students traded sexually explicit memes and messages that sometimes targeted minority groups in a private Facebook group chat.

In the group, students sent memes and other images mocking sexual assault, the Holocaust, and the deaths of children, according to screenshots of the chat obtained by The Crimson. Some messages joked that abusing children was sexually arousing, while others had punchlines directed at specific ethnic or racial groups. One called the hypothetical hanging of a Mexican child, "piñata time."

"The Admissions Committee was disappointed to learn that several students in a private group chat for the Class of 2021 were sending messages that contained offensive messages and graphics," reads a copy of the Admissions Office's email obtained by The Crimson. "As we understand you were among the members contributing such material to this chat, we ask that you submit a statement by tomorrow at noon to explain your contributions and actions for discussion with the Admissions Committee."

"It is unfortunate that I have to reach out about this situation," the email reads.

"As a reminder, Harvard College reserves the right to withdraw an offer of admission under various conditions, including if an admitted student engages in behavior that brings into question his or her honesty, maturity, or moral character," the description reads.

Luca said she had mixed feelings about the administration's move to revoke admissions offers. She said she was "going back and forth" on the matter.

"On the one hand, I think people can post whatever they want because they have the right to do that," Luca said. "I don't think the school should have gone in and rescinded some offers because it wasn't Harvard-affiliated. It was people doing stupid stuff."

She added that if memes sent over the chat posed any kind of threat to members' lives or well-being, then she believed administrators' actions were justified.

"I appreciate humor, but there are so many topics that just should not be joked about," Zhang wrote. "I respect the decision of the admissions officers to rescind the offers because those actions really spoke about the students' true characters."

Question: What is your opinion regarding Harvard's statement:

- "As a reminder, Harvard College reserves the right to withdraw an offer of admission under various conditions, including if an admitted student engages in behavior that brings into question his or her honesty, maturity, or moral character,"

Question: What is your opinion regarding these comments:

- "On the one hand, I think people can post whatever they want because they have the right to do that," Luca said. "I don't think the school should have gone in and rescinded some offers because it wasn't Harvard-affiliated. It was people doing stupid stuff."

- "I appreciate humor, but there are so many topics that just should not be joked about," Zhang wrote. "I respect the decision of the admissions officers to rescind the offers because those actions really spoke about the students' true characters.

Case Study II

A high school football team has an athlete who is homeless. When the coach finds out, he offers the athlete a place to live with him and his family. The athlete accepts. At the end of the player's senior year football season, the team wins a state champion. The athlete is highly recruited by multiple colleges and followed by NFL recruiters.

Case Study III

Controversy from two choices

In a state basketball tournament, two teams are scheduled to play on the school's home court, that is, the higher seed. The host team is located in a predominately Black neighborhood, while the other team is predominately white with a diverse team. One of the top players from the guest team posted racial slurs about the host team on the internet, which the media picked up before the game was played. The player from the guest team was suspended from the game.

The high school association decided to move the game to a different location with a larger seating capacity. The host school had 450 seats and the new location has 1,100 seats. The community surrounding the host gym was upset and said the change was being made because the guest team did not want to play in their neighborhood.

Case Study IV

A car travels behind a school bus on a two-lane roadway through a neighborhood with yellow lines in both directions. The speed limit is thirty-five mph, and the bus has several scheduled stops on this long stretch. It is slowing to make a planned stop for pickup. Just as the bus driver releases the stop sign, the car's driver chooses to increase speed to get around the bus and hits a car in the other lane head-on, causing a fatality.

Case Study V

Members of a high school drumline at a charter school thought the middle school band students should have a drumline. The high school students approached the band director with the suggestion. This idea was new, so he charged the group to work out the details and bring him a solution. The group presented a solution that included members from the high school drumline volunteering to stay after school and work with the students from the middle school band. The band instructor accepted and implemented the solution.

How many choices were made in this case study?

Case Study VI

A daycare employee with a toddler became upset with a supervisor during her assigned shift. When the employee finished the work shift and went home, she went online to vent her frustration concerning the supervisor. The following day, the employee arrived at work to learn that the internet post cost her the job.

Case Study VII

A teen was selected for a summer employment program. The program's positions included various nonprofits and businesses for exposure to different careers. Once training was completed, the teen acknowledged understanding the job duties. After beginning the new position, the teen chose to use the cell phone during working hours instead of doing the work for which she was being paid. This happened multiple times, and eventually, she was terminated.

Case Study VIII

Select a choice you made and analyze it using the same process as the case studies. Identify any ripple effect.

After completing the case studies, what are your observations? What did you learn about making choices?

COMMUNICATION

Principle: Everything Speaks

Communication is a soft skill and can be verbal and nonverbal. It is crucial in all areas of life. The family influences the initial ability to communicate, and the development of communication styles and methods occurs as one grows and interacts with others outside of the primary family group. The interaction will also introduce new cultures and may require behavior modification. For example, an only child may learn to share in a daycare environment.

"Everything speaks" means messages can be stated without words. Someone's behavior, body language, and facial expression can send a louder message without the person ever speaking a word. Customers who interpret a message through a nonverbal encounter will support another store or business. Particularly if they consider the servicer rude or not welcoming. Their message is that "they do not know how to treat their customers." This example of nonverbal communication is real. Losing customers is not what employers want or need to happen. Customers are lost business and will communicate the experience with friends and family through word-of-mouth.

Communication consists of language and speech. Language is words and systems to a people, community, culture, and nation. Language systems are signs and symbols of a specific group, such as fraternities, sororities, or organizations. Because some words do not have a universal meaning such as jargon and specialized vocabulary used by a group or profession, communication can be hampered.

Sometimes written communication is necessary, which requires reading, writing, and a vocabulary. These are basic skills that should be mastered during school matriculation. In the work environment, written reports, business letters, and meeting notes are just a few examples of written communications. Job descriptions may include effective communication as a required skill in certain positions. In the work environment, it is vital to determine what communication method to use in different situations. An email instead of a phone call may not be the best choice if an immediate answer is needed.

What distortions or filters would be barriers to interpretation in the table below?

Example – culture.

Communication Process

Sender	Noise Zone or Barriers to understanding Possible distortions	Receiver
Initiates message		Interprets message

Principle: The Only Person You Can Control Is You

The only person you can control is you. We cannot make someone like us, love us, encourage us, or fulfill an unmet need. Our control occurs through self-management and discipline. Control is another area for choices that is followed by behavior. The outcomes are still either positive or negative. Sometimes people attempt to play the blame game. Blaming someone else does not transfer ownership and responsibility of choice. One's choices reveal beliefs, character, integrity, and values. These attributes shape attitude.

Your attitude is a choice. It is a mental disposition; a feeling or position regarding people or something. It influences the reactions or responses to life's situations and the navigation process. Beginning here helps with understanding the positivity and negativity displayed throughout life. The first pause is in how do you interpret this principle: My attitude will propel me or derail me. It's my choice. Take it a step further and ask someone you know and trust to describe your attitude after self-assessment. Are you surprised by what was said? Did the other descriptions match your description?

Your attitude is crucial because it forms a symbolic lens through which you process life. It comes with ownership and responsibility. Dr. Morton, author of *Defined by Attitude,* states, "Your attitude impacts your thoughts, which impacts your actions, which creates outcomes, which hold consequences." He notes it as a reoccurring cycle. Life will have many situations and challenges that are unexpected and cannot be controlled. In these instances, it's about reacting or responding, and one's attitude will influence how they go about doing so.

This is the synergy and interdependency of the skills because completeness means multiple skills are needed to move forward. You do not leave your integrity at home when you leave because wherever you go, you take you. These soft and life skills will be evident in selecting friends and other relationships.

Actual characteristics will manifest in group settings.

CONFLICT - RESPONSE VS. REACTION

Learning Objectives:

1. Understand conflict is not always negative
2. Response vs. Reaction
3. Understand a person can only control self
4. Another area of choices and consequences

A conflict is a disagreement that can be positive or negative depending on the context. It exists in families, society, work environments, schools, government, and relationships. Different perspectives may work to produce positive outcomes in processes or create improvements. Conflict is experienced early in life in the family environment and continues throughout. The challenge is to learn how to respond and deal with conflict responsibly rather than react. Primarily because reactive behavior is impulsive, and there is no thought process and no self-control. Words spoken and actions taken in the heat of the moment cannot be erased or undone. Harsh words and actions accelerate the situation and make things worse. Many times, reaction leaves negative ripple effects.

Responsive behavior is thoughtful and couples with self-control and discipline. Manage your emotions. You only have control of yourself. Understand your motives. Language and tone mean a lot in any given conversation. Take a time out moment. If necessary, arrange for a neutral person to participate in the discussion. Determine what you want as an outcome and keep in mind, you will not resolve all conflicts, and at times, you may have to agree to disagree.

Understand that control of others may be limited or nonexistent. Sometimes remaining silent is the best option to defuse a situation. Employers have policies and some conflicts require a mediator for resolution.

CONFLICT EXERCISE

Think of a time when you were involved in a conflict and answer the following questions relating to that experience.

What was the disagreement?

_____

_____

_____

_____

Was that the real issue?

_____

_____

_____

_____

Did you contribute to the conflict? If yes, how?

_____

_____

_____

_____

Did you personalize a situation that should not have been?

_____

_____

_____

_____

Did you add something to the situation that was not there?

_____

_____

_____

_____

Did you misunderstand the situation?

_____

_____

_____

_____

Discuss the outcome of the disagreement.

_____

_____

_____

_____

MODULE 2: THE EMPLOYMENT PROCESS

Learning Objectives

1. Identify skill development through volunteerism
2. Understand how to complete an application
3. Identify appropriate references
4. Create a resume
5. Compare the application and resume

Module Description

Entering the workplace for the first time or changing employers can simultaneously be exciting and anxiety-inducing. The content in this section is to assist in the preparation and highlight critical points in the process.

Module Content

Everything speaks throughout the hiring process. Verbal and nonverbal messages are transmitted, whether intentional or unintentional. There is only ONE opportunity to make a first impression.

Getting started...

Know what position you are seeking.

Positions have specific essential functions that a company seeks to fill aligned with its objectives and needs. Detailed qualifications and skills define the jobs. The employment application will request the position for which you are applying. Writing the word "any" in this section is inappropriate because the employer does not have a position known as "any." Instead, take the time to identify and research the companies that have the position you are seeking. Use what you learn to complete the application.

Before accepting a job offer, consider location, transportation, and availability for scheduling. Companies may have similar products and services, but the culture and work environment differ significantly. Create a list of questions to ask if there is an interview.

If there is prior work history, include employer name, address, contact number, dates of employment, supervisor, position held, and duties. If there is no previous work history, volunteerism may serve to show skill development. Include similar information for your voluteer services as what is listed for prior work experience. Create a list of three to five persons for a reference list (no friends or relatives). Ask those selected for permission to use as a reference. The reference section on the application should include the name, address, and contact information.

The Application

An employment application is a tool used in the recruiting process by employers. The application is a non-verbal introduction to the prospective employer. It is the first impression, therefore, it must be completed carefully.

> Do not leave blank spaces.
>
> If handwritten, be neat.
>
> Have two pens in the event writing is necessary.
>
> Spell words correctly, written or typed.
>
> Provide accurate and factual information.

During the screening process, any blank spaces will nullify the consideration of a candidate. Empty spaces may send a variety of non-verbal messages, which may be indicative of how one works or an inattention to details. Irrelevant areas should note "not applicable" (N/A). The notation lets the reviewer know the space was not misunderstood or ignored.

The Resume

A resume is also a nonverbal tool for an individual seeking employment to address a specific position. It is also a nonverbal introduction to the employer. The individual selects the format and determines what information will appear first. There is some flexibility with the resume format. Set up a professional email address.

Chronological vs. Functional

A chronological format lists the work history beginning with current or most recent employment, which aligns more with an application. A functional resume focuses on skills and experience. A person with a graduate degree may decide to list education before work experience. The information should include work, education, skills, and accomplishments regardless of the chosen format.

Employment Application vs. Resume

The difference between the two is that the application is the information required by the employer. The basic information on the application and resume is the same. However, the application contains a section at the end that gives the employer permission to do a background check and speak with references. The applicant's signature also indicates an understanding that any application falsification or background check can lead to immediate termination if hired. If a resume piques interest for the next steps in the hiring process, the applicant completes an application because the resume is missing the language the employer needs.

APPLICATION FOR EMPLOYMENT

Answer all questions

XYZ is an Equal Opportunity Employer. Employment decisions are made based on merit, experience, and other work-related criteria without regard to race, creed, color, religious belief, sex, age, national origin, ancestry, disability, marital status, veteran status, or any other consideration made unlawful by applicable federal, state, or local laws.

Personal Data – PLEASE PRINT CLEARLY	
Name (Last, First, Middle)	Date:
Address (Street, P. O. Box)	Social Security Number:
City/State/Zip	
Home Telephone	Alternate Phone / Email address
Are you authorized to work in the United States? (Verification and completion of Form I-9 must be submitted no later than three business days after the date of hire.) ☐ Yes ☐ No	
Have you been employed by XYZ? ☐ Yes ☐ No	Have you applied with XYZ? ☐Yes ☐ No
Do you have any relatives working at XYZ? ☐ Yes ☐ No If yes, whom? Relationship:	
How did you hear about XYZ?	

Employment Data	
Position Applying For:	Are you willing to work overtime? ☐Yes ☐ No Weekends? ☐Yes ☐ No
Type of Position Desired (check one) ☐Full Time ☐ Part-time	

Date Available to Start:	Desired Salary:

Have you signed an agreement with any other employer that would restrict you from working with XYZ? ☐Yes ☐ No

If yes, explain:

Employment History

List your work history, starting with your current or last employer. You may attach a resume. However, please answer all questions on the application. You may include any verifiable work performed on a volunteer basis, internships, or cooperative education assignments. Note any periods of unemployment. If additional space is required, continue on a separate sheet of paper. Do not attach a resume as a substitute.

Company Name:		Address (City, State, Zip):
Job Title:		Telephone Number:
Start Date:	Start Salary:	Name of Supervisor:
End Date:	Final Salary:	
Reason for leaving:		
Job duties and responsibilities:		
May we contact this employer? ☐Yes ☐No		

Employment History

List your work history, starting with your current or last employer. You may attach a resume. However, please answer all questions on the application. You may include any verifiable work performed on a volunteer basis, internships, or cooperative education assignments. Note any periods of unemployment. If additional space is required, continue on a separate sheet of paper. Do not attach a resume as a substitute.

Company Name:	Address (City, State, Zip):
Job Title:	Telephone Number:
Start Date: Start Salary:	Name of Supervisor:
End Date: Final Salary:	
Reason for leaving:	
Job duties and responsibilities:	
May we contact this employer? ☐Yes ☐No	

Employment History

List your work history, starting with your current or last employer. You may attach a resume. However, please answer all questions on the application. You may include any verifiable work performed on a volunteer basis, internships, or cooperative education assignments. Note any periods of unemployment. If additional space is required, continue on a separate sheet of paper. Do not attach a resume as a substitute.

Company Name:	Address (City, State, Zip):
Job Title:	Telephone Number:

Start Date:	Start Salary:	Name of Supervisor:
End Date:	Final Salary:	
Reason for leaving:		
Job duties and responsibilities:		
May we contact this employer? ☐Yes ☐No		

List any additional skills that you feel qualify you for the job for which you are applying:

Education

	School Name	Location (City and State)	Graduate Yes / No	Degree/Major
High School				
College				
Graduate School				
Business/Trade School				

References

Include the name, phone number, and circumstances of three references, excluding relatives and friends.

Reference Name	
Telephone Number	Length of time known

Reference Name	
Telephone Number	Length of time known

Reference Name	
Telephone Number	Length of time known

Applicant Affirmation

I certify that all the information given by me is true, accurate, and complete. I understand that any omission, misrepresentation, or falsification of any information on this application or supporting documents will result in disqualification from consideration for employment or immediate discharge if employed.

I authorize XYZ to obtain confirmation of all statements contained in this application and/or supporting documents as it relates to the position I am seeking. I release from liability the Company and its representative for seeking such information and all other persons, corporations, or organizations furnishing such information.

I acknowledge that I have read and understand the above statements.

Applicant Signature: _____ Date: _____

Benjamin Z. Zipp

777 Go Court, Orlando, FL 11111
Home phone: 423-999-4399 | Cell phone: 423-888-8088
email address: bzzipp:@gmail.com

Technician II

Professional Skills

Dependable
Good communication skills
Team oriented
Retail customer service
Organizational and planning
Self-motivated
Licensed forklift operator
Inventory stocking
Loading and unloading trucks, planes
Loading equipment operation
Record maintenance
Training
Computer: Microsoft Office package

Employment History

ABC Car Care, January 2015 – present
Position: Technician
Essential duties: Oil change, perform vehicle diagnostic tests.

XYZ Auto Parts – Distribution Center, Wilmington, NC, September 2012 – December 2015
Position: Warehouse Specialist
Essential duties: Pulling orders, loading and unloading trucks, processing returns issuing customer credits, service will-call customers, and inventory stocking.

Education:

Nascar Technical Institute, Mooresville, NC (2014-2015)
Somewhere Community College, Orlando, FL (2007-2008)

Linda Z. Somebody

7340 Anywhere Court • Chicago, IL 28269

341-555-444 • lzsomebody@gmail.com

CAREER SUMMARY

Non-clinical healthcare professional with more than 15 years of experience as a Patient Account Rep, Senior Biller, Claims Benefit Senior Analyst, Rotational Manager, and Customer Service Associate in the industry. Strengths include root cause analysis, process improvement, and interpersonal relations skills.

EDUCATION

Master of Business Administration in Healthcare Management
University of Chicago, Chicago, IL

Bachelor of Arts in Business Administration
Chicago State, Chicago, IL

PROFESSIONAL DEVELOPMENT

Inducted into the National Society of Leadership and Success (Summer 2021)

Certified Six Sigma Green Belt (completion August 2012)
Somewhere Community College, Chicago, IL

Certificate for Medical Billing and Coding (completion December 2010)
Somewhere Community College, Charlotte, NC

TECHNICAL SKILLS

MS Office
Epic

PROFESSIONAL EXPERIENCE

BCBS Health, Chicago, IL • January 2019-Present

Patient Account Rep/CSR/PFS

Provide excellent communications with collection agencies, patients, attorneys, insurance community in a high-paced environment. Partner with other departments to process requests to completion. Document all pertinent information of an account in the appropriate software. Initiate monthly payment contract on accounts. Inform leadership of problems along with possible solutions.

- Met call metrics for 15 continuous months.
- Met QA 6 months

Customer Service Advisory Council

- Team representative to the council to communicate the needs and concerns of the staff.
- Coordinate as a liaison within the department, director of the department, assistant vice president, and occasionally to other teams as needed.
- Create and organize programs and projects.
- Served turn as acting secretary for the month.

ABC Health, Chicago, IL • March 2013-June 2017

Senior Biller

- Collected $11,000 of outstanding balances on aged accounts.
- Subject Matter Expert for Workers Compensation.
- Proposed a new strategy for Workers' Compensation.
- Resolve Claim Edit daily ranging from $6000-$15,000.
- Created a Workers Comp tip sheet for teammates.
- Collaborated with site and payer. Collected outstanding balance of $6000 on the aged account.
- Presented workflow strategy, implemented to reduce rising AR.
- Achieved Gold Standard on One Score for more than 18 months.
- Identified system coding error that was corrected by management, reducing reimbursement delay.
- Participated in creating SOP for insurance follow-up.
- 1 of 5 out of 18 selected to lead the project.
- Resolved compliance issues.

WXYD, Chicago, IL • 2002–March 2013

Claims Benefit Senior Analyst (2004–2013)

- Earned several WXYD Champion Awards.
- Achieved MVP award for outstanding quality and production.
- Attained Service Counts Award for meeting silver and gold production and quality standards.
- Awarded several certificates for 100% Quality for a Month Conducted root-cause analysis.

- Assist in front-line claims on an as-needed basis.
- Reconcile refund/reversals on claim payment systems.
- Delivered reduction in the amount of aged inventory by adjusting workflow patterns.
- Generated meeting metrics/goals through solid leadership and cultivation of team environment.
- Orchestrate communication with administrators on assigned accounts.

Rotational Manager (2006)

Managed 18 personnel. Directed day-to-day operations concerning inventory and daily reports and aided processors in achieving production and quality standards. Oversaw workflow to maintain processors' workload.

- Achieved lowest high-dollar inventory through strategic planning with upper management, calculating daily receipts, and reallocating resources based on amounts.
- Drove a high customer satisfaction rate by working closely with internal partners to establish workflows that ensured meeting customer standards.
- Implemented results-oriented culture by assigning receipts to personnel according to their scope of work and rewarding them for their accomplishments.
- Earned WXYD Champion Award.

Before You Go:

- Research the company
- Know the position you are applying for
- Create a reference list of 3 peoople that are not relatives
    - Ask each person for permission to use them as a reference
- Get the correct information: name, address, contact information
- Mute or turn off your cell phone

The Interview

There is only one opportunity to make a first impression! Communication during the interview is both verbal and nonverbal. Because appearance is the first thing noticed, an image is made within ten seconds of initial contact. Some interviewers may determine the time allotted to interview during that first ten seconds. Make a great first impression.

There is a shift to a more casual approach to interview attire. Some companies are scheduling virtual interviews. While there may be resistance to the recommended attire, the first impression is still on the table and will be made. There should not be a difference in attitude and choice between an in-person or virtual interview. The priority is the interview. Your attire is your choice and control, and the interview method is not in your control. This is an example of the interdependency of skills.

Some companies may be more relaxed with interview attire, but this is where researching the company is essential. Also, ask the person scheduling the interview for guidance on attire requirements if you are unsure. Even in a relaxed environment, there is only one opportunity to make the first impression. Attire should not be a distraction during the interview. The focus should be on the skills and experience that the applicant brings.

Interview Attire

<u>Women</u>

Business suit: solid navy, dark gray, or black

Coordinated blouse

If wearing a skirt, it should be no more than 1 inch above the knee

Closed-toe shoes with 1-2 inch heels

Neat, professional hairstyle, subtle makeup

Limited jewelry

Folio: include extra resumes and a pen

No large earrings or an arm full of bracelets

<u>Men</u>

Business suit: solid navy, dark gray, or black

White dress shirt or color-coordinated with suit

Tie

Dark socks, conservative shoes

Neat, professional hair

Folio: include extra resumes and a pen

Everyone

Avoid heavy perfume and cologne

No gum, coffee, or soda

If you have several piercings, consider leaving some of your jewelry at home

If possible, cover tattoos

Avoid jeans and overly casual clothing

Attire Don'ts

Short hemlines	Evening party attire
Tight clothing	Leggings
Sweatsuits	Heavy makeup
Flip Flops	T-shirts
Jumpsuits	Uniforms from another company
Denim	Muscle shirts
Low cut tops	Sagging pants

Interview appointment

Interviews are usually multilevel, consisting of supervisors, managers, and human resources.

Sometimes there may be a group interview or it is a one-on-one interview. The structure differs from company to company.

After the interview, always send (via email or by regular mail) a thank-you note.

Suggested Exercises

According to research, employers indicate that soft skills are lacking. Employment is very different from school and home. Create opportunities for participants to stand and present orally throughout training.

Plan mock interviews by asking professional human resource personnel to come and assist. Complete a rating sheet and review with the participant to identify areas for improvement.

MODULE 3: MONEY MANAGEMENT

Learning Objectives

1. Create a budget
2. Understand income, expense, and disposal income
3. Analyze how choices affect money management
4. Explain debt
5. Discuss emergencies
6. Introduction to Entrepreneurship

Vocabulary:

1. **Debt** – borrowed money for the purchase of something, must be repaid, a liability
2. **Wage** – money paid for work or services, paid hourly, daily, weekly, bi-weekly, monthly, or bi-monthly
3. **Disposable income** – (net income) the amount remaining after deducting personal income taxes from wages
4. **Budget** – an itemized estimate of expected income and expenses for a given period in the future

Module Description

The module is intended to identify the synergy of life skills: education, learning, and employment for life application. Daily living is the culmination of education, formal, and informal learning.

Congratulations! You are employed. For the following exercises, however, the wage is $7.75 per hour. That is the federal minimum wage paid for work.

The interview is complete. The internal selection conversation has taken place, and you are hired. The employer ran a background check and spoke to listed references. At this point, your profile passed. Now you are adding work experience to your profile which may be new skills since this is a new job. The better and more robust your profile, the better your opportunities are for advancing. Now that there is income, we will look at the expense of transportation and a place to live. After a separate analysis of each, comes the budget. The budget may include other expenses outside of these two items.

The following exercise captures the expenses associated with vehicle ownership and having an apartment. If the vehicle is a cash purchase, there is no down payment. If a loan is needed, there is a down payment and a credit check. A credit check is a history showing how a person paid bills, whether there were late payments and how much debt the person has—a different area of choice. A person is denied if the credit check is not good.

Fill in the amounts of exercises one and two by using a pay of $7.75 an hour and a 40-hour work week. Once the amounts are completed, choose whether it's a "go" or "no go."

Exercise 1: Vehicle Purchase and Maintenance Budget

Item	Amount	Monthly Payment	Weekly Expense
Car price			
Down payment			
Insurance			
Tag			

Maintenance

Gas			
Oil Change			
Tires			
Repairs			
Property tax (yearly)			
Tag renewal (yearly)			
Inspection (yearly)			

Exercise 2: First Apartment + 6 Months Of Expenses

	Move-In	Jan	Feb	Mar	Apr	May	Jun	July
Security deposit								
Rent								
Water								
Electricity								
Gas								
Cable								
Food								

Phone							
Insurance							
Clothes							
Transportation							

Exercise 3: Student Choice

Identify the purchase of a need or want and list anything associated with the purchase and any maintenance, if any. That is the total cost.

Additional Cost	Need	Need Cost	Want	Want Cost
1.				
2.				
3.				

Budget

A budget helps track money earned and received, income, and spending, including rent, food, utility bills, and phone. If expenses and debts total more than income, a solution is to increase income, reduce spending, or both.

Spending has two groups, need and want. During cold weather, a coat is a need. However, a specific designer coat is a want.

Complete the following budget exercises using a salary of $7.75 per hour and a 40-hour work week. Students will have a realistic experience of planning how to live on minimum wage.

Budget Items

Income/Savings	Amounts	Monthly	Quarterly	Annual
#1				
#2				
Savings				
Emergency Savings				
Bills/Expenses	Amounts	Monthly	Quarterly	Annual

Rent				
Transportation				
Food				
Utilities				
Clothes				
Medical				

MODULE 4: SELF-MANAGEMENT

After completing this lesson, you will:

1. Understand time management does not exist
2. Examine how you use your time
3. List the areas of wasted time
4. Develop a plan for improvement

When you are not as productive as needed, or you miss a deadline, you may be told to manage your time, or you need to learn how to manage your time. It sounds reasonable, but the fallacy is that time is not manageable. Let's break it down.

Manage is "to dominate, influence, handle, direct, or control." Time is fixed, sixty seconds is a minute, sixty minutes is an hour, twenty-four hours is a day, seven days in a week, and so on. Once it has passed, it is gone. There are no start, pause, and rewind buttons to press with time. The implication that time can somehow be controlled or manipulated is misleading as we cannot "manage" time.

Since time is the same for all, how is it that some people can accomplish more than others? The answer is self-management – **managing choices**, intentional awareness of priorities, and focus. The ability to control, dominate, influence, and govern does apply to self. Each individual is the steward of their time and **chooses** the use. This is another area where the words control and choice show up and contribute to the "profile."

Some excuses and reasons are given for not accomplishing as much as desired. Many of these reasons are time busters such as procrastination, over-commitment, clutter, unexpected interruptions (not always a negative), lack of planning, a false sense of confidence, fear, overconfidence, TV, video games, social media, and whatever else gets tagged priority whether intentional or not. Time busters are chosen behaviors that come with a price. Costs include: missed opportunities, rushing and producing poor quality, not achieving full potential, character development, discipline, dependability, and accountability.

Efficiency and productivity come with a shift in the cycle addressed earlier in the control principle. The cycle is Attitude → Thoughts → Actions → Outcome → Consequences. Take a minute, consider how you currently use your time, and make a list. The list is your priority. If your list is not helping your productivity, an intentional shift can help you.

People have different functional roles (athlete, teacher, student, employee, leader, etc.). The roles are interdependent because the person is central in each. Each role has different responsibilities and accountability. Identify and understand each role that applies to you. Volunteer and organization membership should also be noted because they are commitments made.

Making The Shift To Self-Management

- Identify the priority of each role. Some priorities may have deadlines. For example, a student may have a school project due on a specific date or a test.

- Organize and set clear and specific goals for each.

- Write them down, plan your week, and keep a list to stay focused and on point.

- Get rid of clutter wherever it is in your life. Clutter is a distraction and impedes productivity. It can be physical and/or mental. Wading through clutter takes more time and energy to complete a task and may cause frustration and anxiety.

- There are occasions when saying no is appropriate. Understand obligations and responsibilities holistically.

- Create checkpoints and evaluations to determine if adjustments are needed if and when things change.

- Know when to say *no*

- Do not major in the minors. Everything is not a priority so know what is important and what is not

- Choose your battles wisely. Do not get drawn into other people's agendas, motives, and drama. Do not permit others to hijack your time. Create and protect boundaries.

- When life happens, and it will, the ability to re-evaluate, reprioritize, and reallocate resources is a better response than attempting to do something impossible - managing time.

- Make time for rest and relaxation. Turn off the cell phone, close the computer, and relax. Self-care is part of self-management. Take care of your mind, body, soul, and spirit. A healthy awareness is essential for efficiency and healthy living.

As a challenge, focus on making positive behavioral shifts that will impact your profile.

SELF-MANAGEMENT ASSESSMENT

High energy: ____A.M.   ____P.M.

Time Busters:

Check all that apply and if something is not listed, add it.

√	Time Buster	Why is this a buster	Cost
	Procrastination		
	Over Commitment		
	Clutter		
	Unexpected interruptions		
	Lack of planning		
	Social media		
	TV		
	False sense of confidence		
	Fear		
	Cell phone		
	Phone calls		
	Video games, Computer		

I spend most of my time doing:

_____

_____

The time buster(s) I want to change most is:

_____

_____

Identify roles and responsibilities

In the below table, indicate deadline order in the far left column.

	Roles	Priorities	Due Date

PROFILE CHECK-UP

What would the report contain if a background and reference check were processed within the next two days? Sometimes it is essential to stop and self-evaluate to ensure you are on the path you desire to be on or, if not, make adjustments. Past choices cannot be undone, but learning and moving forward can. This is a check-up.

My Attitude will propel (positive forward movement) me or derail me. It's my choice.

Do I tend to look for the positive or the negative in people or situations, and why?

Do I feel a responsibility to improve the lives of others?

Do I take complete responsibility for my own attitude?

What do I believe and value?

Are my beliefs easily swayed or influenced by external factors?

Do I have negotiables and non-negotiables?

Do I have boundaries?

Am I influenced and impacted by social media?

How do I make choices? Do I think about the consequences?

Am I able to leave a harmful and toxic situation or environment?

Do I ask for help when I need it? Why or why not?

What adjustments do I need to make to my self-management?

Am I effective in my communication? Am I willing to get opinions from others?

What is the tone of my communication?

Do I have what it takes to own a business?

I will be the boss, and I will be my most important employee. Can I handle it?

Am I self-motivated?

How do I handle rejection?

How do I make decisions?

How *well* do I make decisions?

Do I plan and am I organized?

Am I task-oriented or people-oriented?

How well do I get along with different cultures and ethnicities?

Do I have support from my family?

Would I hire someone like me?

What is my work ethic?

Is there anything on my Self-Management Assessment that is a potential problem?

RESOURCES

www.indeed.com/career-advice/resumes-cover-letters/soft-skills

Mitchell, G. W., Skinner, L. B., & White, B. J. (2010). Essential Soft Skills For Success In The Twenty-First Century Workforce As Perceived By Business Educators. *Delta Pi Epsilon Journal,* *52*(1), 43-53. Retrieved from https://search.proquest.com/docview/288422382?accountid=40162

Morton, K., *Defined by Attitude: The Power of Positivity,* 2021.

www.dictionary.com

http://wdr.doleta.gov/SCANS/idsrw.pdf

https://www.thebalancecareers.com/interview